HOWARD JUNIOR SCHOOL

Removed
CT

Dragon's Lost Roar

by Julia Rawlinson

Illustrated by Beccy Blake

W

FRANKLIN WATTS

LONDON•SYDNEY

About this book

Rhymes to Read are designed for children who are ready to start reading alone. They can also be used by an adult to share with a child.

The books provide excellent support for developing phonological awareness helping the child to recognise sounds and sound-symbol relationships. The poems are perfect to read aloud and the strong rhythms, rhymes and repetition will help build confidence and encourage reading and rereading for pleasure.

Reading tips for adults sharing the book with a child:

1. Make reading fun! Choose a time to read when you and the child are relaxed and have time to share the story.
2. Talk about the story before you start reading. Look at the cover and the blurb. What might the story be about? Why might the child like it?
3. Encourage the child to retell the story, using the pictures and rhymes to help. The puzzles at the back of the book provide a good starting point.
4. Give praise! Remember that small mistakes need not always be corrected.
5. For an extra activity, you could ask the child to make up some alternative rhyme for the story or their own brand new rhyme!

Dragon woke and stretched his wings, and said, "I feel like eating things."

3

I'd better check
my scary noise."

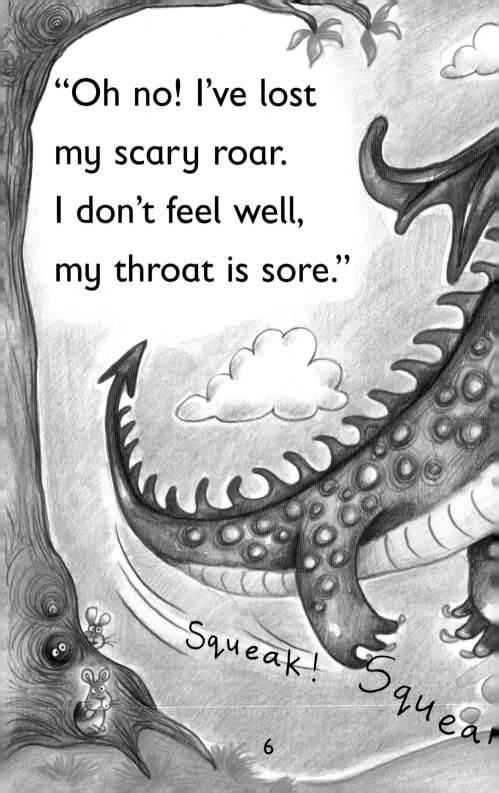

"Oh no! I've lost
my scary roar.
I don't feel well,
my throat is sore."

Squeak! Squea

6

He ran to Witch,
who said she'd brew

8

something to make him

good as new.

She handed him
her cooking pot.

10

He held his nose
and drank the lot.

His ears caught fire.

His eyes span round.

12

His tummy made

a funny sound!

hic!

hic!

hic!

13

"Oh dear!" said Witch.
"You need a fright."
So she conjured up
a scary sight ...

15

Some giant girls
and giant boys,
laughing at Dragon's
funny noise.

17

The children scared
away his hics.

At last, his scary roar
was fixed!

But Dragon now felt
quite worn out,

and a different sound
came from his snout!

Puzzle 1

Put the pictures in the correct
order and retell the story.

Puzzle 2

lost

well

sore

roar

snout

snore

sound

out

Find the rhyming words above.

Turn over for answers!

Answers

Puzzle 1

The correct order is: b, a, c.

Puzzle 2

The rhyming words are:

a. roar, sore

b. out, snout

First published in 2011 by
Franklin Watts
338 Euston Road
London
NW1 3BH

Franklin Watts Australia
Level 17/207 Kent Street
Sydney
NSW 2000

Text © Julia Rawlinson 2011
Illustration © Beccy Blake 2011

The rights of Julia Rawlinson to be
identified as the author and Beccy Blake
as the illustrator of this Work have been
asserted in accordance with the Copyright,
Designs and Patents Act, 1988.

A CIP catalogue record for this book is
available from the British Library.

ISBN 978 1 4451 0295 5 (hbk)
ISBN 978 1 4451 0302 0 (pbk)

Series Editor: Melanie Palmer
Series Advisor: Catherine Glavina
Series Designer: Peter Scoulding

Printed in China

Franklin Watts is a division of Hachette Children's Books,
an Hachette UK company. www.hachette.co.uk